JOHN SCHNEIDER

The True Story Of How A Small-town Boy Country Music Legend Became A Hollywood Star And A Candid Account Of His Success, Struggle And Survival

Mia Publications

COPYRIGHT ©2023 BY MIA PUBLICATIONS
All Rights Reserved
No part of this book may be reproduced, distributed, or transmitted in any form or by any means including photocopying, recording, or other electronic or mechanical methods without the prior written permission of the publisher, except in the case of brief quotations embodied in critical reviews and certain other non-commercial uses permitted by copyright laws.

DISCLAIMER

This book is written for informational purposes only. The information presented is without contract or any type of guarantee assurance. Also, this book is not sponsored by or affiliated with John Schneider, it is only a detailed biography from reliable close sources.

While every caution has been taken to provide accurate and current information, it is solely the reader's responsibility to check all information contained in this book before relying upon it.

Neither the author nor publisher can be held accountable for any errors or omissions. Under no circumstances will any legal responsibility or blame be held against the author or publisher for any reparation, damages, or monetary loss due to the information presented, either directly or indirectly.

TABLE OF CONTENTS

FOREWORD..**5**
CHAPTER ONE..**8**
  The Early Years..*8*
CHAPTER TWO..**14**
  The Breakthrough....................................*14*
CHAPTER THREE..**18**
  The Stardom...*18*
CHAPTER FOUR..**25**
  Into The Hot Soup...................................*25*
CHAPTER FIVE..***30***
  The Comeback..*30*
CHAPTER SIX..**35**
  Inspiring Generations Of Fans And Artists...*35*
CHAPTER SEVEN..**42**
  Rare Fun Facts About John Schneider.*42*

FOREWORD

"Don't let anyone tell you that you can't do it." You must dream high, work hard, and remain humble. And never forget where you've come from." –John Schneider.

If you like country music, Hollywood movies, or TV shows, you've probably heard of John Schneider. He is one of the most varied and successful entertainers of our time, with a four-decade career and numerous honors and accolades. But do you know the whole tale of how he got to be the man he is today?

In this book, you'll learn about John Schneider's incredible journey, from his humble beginnings in a small hamlet in New York to his ascent to stardom as Bo Duke in The Dukes of

Hazzard, to his move to the big screen and the music industry, to his personal and professional problems and victories. You will learn about his drive, tenacity, faith, and family. You'll also get a look at his behind-the-scenes experiences, observations, and guidance for aspiring artists and dreamers.

This work is much more than a biography. It's a candid and uplifting look at how a small-town youngster became a country music icon and a Hollywood celebrity, as well as how he survived and thrived in the entertainment industry. It also demonstrates the power of dreams, the significance of roots, and the value of authenticity.

Whether you've been a fan of John Schneider for a long time or are just interested about him, this book will entertain, enlighten, and motivate you. It will provide answers to your questions regarding his life, career, and legacy. It will also demonstrate why he is one of the entertainment industry's most beloved and respected people.

This book is for everyone who enjoys music, movies, television, or stories about success, failure, and survival. It is intended for everyone who want to benefit from the experiences and knowledge of a legend. It's for anyone who wants to be inspired by the genuine story of how a small-town youngster rose to stardom in Hollywood. This is a book you should not pass up.

CHAPTER ONE

The Early Years

On April 8, 1960, John Richard Schneider IV was born in Mount Kisco, New York, a small village in the Hudson Valley. He was the youngest of three boys born to Shirley Conklin and John Richard "Jack" Schneider III, a pilot and member of the United States Air Force. When his parents split when he was two years old, he moved in with his mother, who supported her children by working as a secretary and a waitress. John had a distant relationship with his father, who remarried and relocated to Colorado. John only saw him on holidays and during summer vacations.

John had a difficult childhood. He had to deal with poverty, bullying, and loneliness. He frequently felt like an outcast because he was one of the few youngsters in his community with divorced parents. He also had dyslexia, a learning handicap that made it difficult for him to read and write. His classmates taunted and mocked him, thinking he was stupid and slow. He had low self-esteem and a defiant personality. He got into fights, missed school, and ran away from home on multiple occasions.

But John had a bright side as well. He was a curious, imaginative, and adventurous young man who enjoyed exploring his surroundings. He was into music, magic, and movies. He learned to play the guitar, harmonica, and piano by himself. He did magic tricks for his friends and family, as well as random strangers on the street. He watched every movie he could get his hands on, including westerns and comedies. He was a fan of actors such as John Wayne, Clint Eastwood, Burt Reynolds, and Steve Martin. He aspired to be a celebrity like them one day.

John's career as a performer began when he was eight years old, when he performed magic performances for his classmates and their families. This once landed him in hot water when he had himself locked up and thrown into a swimming pool with the goal of reenacting Harry Houdini's renowned escape act. He eventually freed himself and swam to the surface, but not before causing his mother a heart attack.

John realized his acting aptitude at a young age as well. He appeared in numerous productions in New York City, where he studied acting and auditioned for various roles. When he was nine years old, he earned his first professional role as a small child in a commercial for a local bank. In addition, he appeared in several off-Broadway musicals, including The King and I, The Sound of Music, and Oliver!

He and his mother moved to Atlanta, Georgia, when he was 14, where his passion for acting flourished. He became interested with the local theater and appeared in a number of local performances. In addition, he founded his own band, John Schneider and the Moonlighters, and performed at numerous places and events. He appeared in Smokey and the Bandit, a 1977 hit starring one of his idols, Burt Reynolds. He was also a popular student and excellent athlete at North Springs High School. He participated in football, basketball, baseball, and track & field. He was voted "Most Likely to Succeed" by his peers.

But John's actual desire was to establish a name for himself in Hollywood. He desired to appear on television and in films, as well as to have millions of fans. He knew he had the beauty, charm, charisma, and talent to succeed. He only needed a chance to show himself. And that opportunity came when he was 18 years old, when he was cast as Bo Duke in a new TV show called The Dukes of Hazzard, opposite newcomer Tom Wopat and veteran actor James Best. It was the start of a new chapter in his life, one that would permanently alter his destiny.

CHAPTER TWO

The Breakthrough

John Schneider had always wanted to be an actor, but he encountered numerous obstacles and rejections along the road. He was born in Mount Kisco, New York, but relocated to Atlanta, Georgia, when he was 14 years old with his mother. He developed an interest in performing and began putting on magic performances for his friends and family. He also learnt to play the guitar and sing, and he became a member of a local theater group.

He tried out for several parts, but none appeared to fit his personality or style. For the casting directors, he was either too tall, too blonde, too young, or too

Southern. He was about to abandon his acting profession when he learned of a new TV show asking for two young actors to play cousins who drive fast cars and fight the corrupt system in a rural region.

The sitcom, The Dukes of Hazzard, was inspired by the 1975 film Moonrunners, which featured real-life moonshiners and bootleggers. The producers intended to develop a show that would appeal to both young and old audiences. They were seeking two actors who could embody the main characters' charm, wit, and bravery, Bo and Luke Duke.

John Schneider decided to give it a chance, and he cleverly prepared for the audition. He knew the filmmakers were looking for genuine Southern actors, so he pretended to be one. He sported a beard, a cowboy hat and boots, and a beer can. He also lied about his age, claiming to be 24 rather than 18. He claimed to be from Snellville, Georgia, and to have raced cars since he was a child.

His enthusiasm and confidence attracted the filmmakers, and he was partnered with another actor, Tom Wopat, who was auditioning for the role of Luke Duke. They had instant connection, and they acted out a scene in which they had to hop into the General Lee, their iconic orange Dodge Charger, and drive away from the sheriff. They did it so skillfully that the automobile smashed into a fence, but they continued to act as if nothing had occurred.

The producers were so impressed with their performance that they decided to cast them as the Duke boys. Bo Duke, the blonde, impetuous, and romantic cousin who loved to drive fast and flirt with the girls, was played by John Schneider. He was pleased and immediately called his mother to inform her of the good news. He'd finally made it, and he was ready to embark on his career as a Hollywood star.

CHAPTER THREE

The Stardom

John Schneider's meteoric career began in 1979, when he was cast as Bo Duke on the blockbuster TV show The Dukes of Hazzard. He was only 18 at the time, and he had to lie about his age and hometown in order to earn the part. During his audition, he pretended to be a true rural boy from Snellville, Georgia, and donned a beard and clutched a beer can. He wowed the producers with his personality and driving abilities, and he quickly became one of America's most popular and known faces.

The Dukes of Hazzard was a comedy-action television series that featured the exploits of the Duke cousins, Bo and Luke, who drove around in their orange 1969 Dodge Charger, nicknamed the General Lee, and frequently got in conflict with the law in their rural county of Hazzard. Catherine Bach played their cousin Daisy Duke, James Best played the foolish Sheriff Rosco P. Coltrane, and Denver Pyle played their smart Uncle Jesse1. The show was a big success, drawing millions of viewers each week and creating a slew of goods, including toys, games, apparel, and even a lunch box. Schneider rose to prominence as a teen idol and a sex symbol, and he relished the benefits of celebrity, such as meeting celebrities, attending parties, and driving fast automobiles.

However, Schneider encountered some issues and challenges during his tenure on the show. He had to deal with the pressures of celebrity, media criticism, and network demands. He also had some disagreements with his co-star Tom Wopat, who played Luke Duke, about their pay and screen time. Schneider and Wopat went on strike and departed the show for a few episodes in 1982, demanding a larger cut of the earnings and greater creative control. They were temporarily replaced by two other actors who represented their cousins Coy and Vance, but the ratings plummeted and fans rioted. Schneider and Wopat eventually returned to the show after reaching an agreement with the producers.

While continuing to work on The Dukes of Hazzard, Schneider sought a career in music, which had been his passion since he was a boy. His mother, a music teacher, had taught him to play the guitar and sing, and he had appeared in several small theater shows in New York and Atlanta. In 1981, he signed with Scotti Brothers Records and released his debut album, Now or Never, which included a cover of Elvis Presley's classic song "It's Now or Never." The song peaked at number four on the Billboard Hot Country Singles chart in 1983, becoming the best-selling single by a solo country singer. Schneider also made history by being the first country musician to have a music video, which was shot at Elvis Presley's Graceland home.

Throughout the 1980s, Schneider continued to record albums and singles, and he rose to become one of the most successful and respected country artists of the decade3. He has 18 singles in the top ten on the country charts, four of which hit number one: "I've Been Around Enough to Know", "Country Girls", "What's a Memory Like You (Doing in a Love Like This)", and "You're the Last Thing I Needed Tonight". He has received multiple honors and nominations, including the Academy of Country Music Award for Top New Male Vocalist in 1982 and a Grammy Award nomination in 1983 for Best Male Country Vocal Performance. He has worked with other musicians, including Marie Osmond, Waylon Jennings, and Willie Nelson, and performed at a variety of places and occasions, including the Grand Ole Opry, the White House, and the Farm Aid concert.

Schneider's musical career also aided his acting career, as he performed in various films and TV episodes that used his singing abilities3. He played a country singer who falls in love with a city girl in the 1982 TV movie Dream House. He also appeared in the 1984 TV movie Eddie Macon's Run as an escaped convict pursued by a ruthless sheriff played by Kirk Douglas. He also appears in the 1987 musical comedy The Curse of the Crystal Eye as a treasure hunter who joins forces with a singer played by Cybill Shepherd. He also provided the voice of a cowboy in the animated film The Legend of the

Ruby Silver, in which he assisted a girl in discovering a fabled mine.

Schneider's popularity and adaptability quickly garnered him the attention and respect of his fans and peers. He has demonstrated that he was more than a nice face and a talented driver, and that he has the talent and ambition to follow his dreams.

CHAPTER FOUR

Into The Hot Soup

Schneider's life was not always easy, as he encountered many challenges and setbacks in his personal and professional life. Among other things, he had to deal with divorce, financial difficulties, legal concerns, and familial estrangement. He also had to deal with the entertainment industry's changing trends and demands, as well as find ways to reinvent himself and stay relevant.

Schneider's first marriage to Tawny Little, a former Miss America, lasted only three years, from 1983 to 19861. They first met at the 1982 Academy Awards, where Little was covering the red carpet and interviewing Schneider.

They began dating a few months later, but their relationship quickly grew rocky due to their hectic schedules and opposing lifestyles. They split amicably and kept in touch.

Schneider's second marriage, from 1993 to 2019, to Elvira "Elly" Castle, was more turbulent and lasted longer. They were the parents of three children, two of whom were from Castle's previous marriage. They also ran a film studio in Louisiana, where they produced and appeared in a number of films and television shows. Their marriage, however, was fraught with tension and arguments, and Castle filed for divorce in 2014, alleging irreconcilable differences.

The divorce was lengthy and contentious, with the couple arguing over alimony, property, and custody. Schneider was ordered to pay $18,000 a month in alimony by the court, but he claimed he couldn't afford it, blaming his enormous debt and financial difficulties. He also stated that he had spent the majority of his money restoring his movie studio, which had been wrecked by a flood in 2016. He failed to make the payments and was repeatedly placed in contempt of court. In 2018, he served a brief jail sentence for owing $150,000 in alimony. After five years of legal wrangling, the divorce was ultimately finalized in 2019.

Schneider's financial difficulties also had an impact on his career, as he struggled to obtain consistent and lucrative work in Hollywood. To finance and release his creations, he had to rely on crowdsourcing and self-distribution. He also had to contend with changing consumer tastes and inclinations, which were more interested in superhero movies and streaming services than in his typical genres of comedy, action, and country music. He attempted to adapt and expand his roles, but he was met with criticism and resentment from some of his supporters who accused him of forsaking his roots and ideals.

Schneider's personal life suffered as a result of his estrangement from his three adult children, who supported their mother in the divorce. He stated that they had stopped speaking to him and refused to see him. He also stated that they disapproved of his new relationship with Alicia Allain, his producing partner and manager, whom he began seeing in 2015. In 2019, he married Allain in a spiritual wedding while still legally married to Castle. He stated that in God's eyes, he was married to Allain and that he wanted to move on with his life.

CHAPTER FIVE

The Comeback

After the death of his wife, Alicia, to cancer in 2023, John Schneider's life was not over. He still had a lot to give the world, and he was determined to respect her memory and legacy by following his aspirations and passions. In his grief, he also relied on his great trust in God and his belief in heaven for hope and solace. He refused to give up and made a tremendous return in both his career and faith.

Schneider's comeback began with his return to the music world, where he launched a number of new albums and singles showcasing his talent and flexibility as a vocalist and composer. He also played at several places and events, including the CMA Fest, the Grand Ole Opry, and the Country Music Hall of Fame. He also established his own record label, Maven Entertainment, as well as his own streaming service, CineFlix, via which he delivered his music and films to his admirers.

Schneider's comeback included reprising his renowned role as Bo Duke in the Dukes of Hazzard franchise, which he developed and starred in since 1979. He created and appeared in various films and television shows that paid homage to the legendary series, including Stand on It!, Poker Run, and Christmas Cars, in which he drove the famed General Lee car and performed stunts and comedy. He also reconnected with previous co-stars

Tom Wopat, Catherine Bach, and James Best, and he recruited new performers Danny Trejo, Barry Corbin, and Dean Cain to join the fun. He frequently attended fan conventions and festivals, such as the Dukes of Hazzard Reunion, where he met and mingled with his devoted fans.

Schneider's comeback also encompassed new genres and roles in the cinema and television industries, where he demonstrated his abilities and ingenuity as an actor, director, producer, and writer. He worked on a variety of projects, including The Haves and the Have Nots, One Month Out, The Stairs, and Jingle Smells, in the drama, thriller, horror, comedy, romance, and action genres. In films like Doonby, October Baby, and The

Reliant, he also explored contentious and tough issues like abortion, racism, and politics. In films such as What Would Jesus Do?, Like Son, and The Confession Musical, he also conveyed his beliefs and principles.

Schneider's comeback also showed his personal growth and maturity, as he handled his difficulties and faults with honesty and humility. He settled his legal and financial disagreements with his ex-wife, Elvira Castle, and paid his obligations and taxes. He also reconnected with his estranged children and welcomed his grandchildren into his life after years of estrangement. He also rediscovered love and happiness with his new wife, Alicia Allain, who was his producing partner and manager prior to their marriage in 2019. He also became closer to God and his church, and he shared his testimony and message of hope and grace with others.

Schneider's comeback was a monument to his perseverance and resolve to conquer adversity. He never let his loss or suffering prevent him from living his life and carrying out his mission. He also never forgot his wife, Alicia, and he continued to produce art and convey joy in her memory and legacy. He never lost his faith or optimism, and he eagerly anticipated the day when he would meet her again in paradise. Many people who respected his talent and enthusiasm saw him as an example of courage and endurance.

CHAPTER SIX

Inspiring Generations Of Fans And Artists

John Schneider is more than a well-known actor and singer. He is also a trendsetter, philanthropist, mentor, and role model for millions of people who respect his talent, charisma, and courage. Schneider's work and life have inspired generations of fans and artists throughout his career, leaving a lasting impression on the entertainment business and society at large.

Schneider's legendary portrayal as Bo Duke in the smash TV program The Dukes of Hazzard is one of the most visible ways he has affected others. From 1979 to 1985, the show was a cultural phenomenon that captured fans with its blend of comedy, action, and family values. Schneider, who was barely 18 at the time of his audition, brought a youthful vitality and charm to the role, making him a cult favorite and a sex symbol. His relationship with co-star Tom Wopat, who played his cousin Luke Duke, was also crucial to the show's success. They produced one of the most iconic TV duos, traveling about in their famed automobile, the General Lee, and outwitting the corrupt officials of Hazzard County.

The Dukes of Hazzard not only amused millions of viewers, but also inspired many aspiring actors and musicians who aspired to be like Schneider. Brad Paisley, Keith Urban, Blake Shelton, and Luke Bryan are among the celebrities who have mentioned Schneider as an inspiration. They all grew up watching the show and admiring Schneider's musical abilities. Schneider, who released multiple albums and had numerous country chart hits, was one of the first actors to successfully transition into the music industry, opening the door for others to follow. He also aided in the popularization of the Southern rock and country genres, which were frequently overlooked by the mainstream media.

Schneider has also influenced people through his performance as Jonathan Kent, Clark Kent's adoptive father, in the TV show Smallville. The show, which aired from 2001 to 2011, was a modern recreation of the Superman origin tale, focused on the future superhero's adolescence. Schneider, who played Clark's moral compass and guiding influence, provided depth and compassion to the character, making him a revered figure among both fans and the performers. Critics and spectators alike praised his portrayal of Jonathan Kent, praising his subtle and realistic performance. Schneider, who lost his father when he was 17 years old, drew on his personal experience to imbue the character with emotion and sincerity.

Smallville not only revitalized Schneider's career, but it also affected a generation of young viewers who grew up watching the program and learnt good things from it. Identity, destiny, friendship, loyalty, love, and sacrifice are some of the topics tackled in the program. Schneider, who served as a mentor and friend to his co-stars, particularly Tom Welling, who played Clark Kent, shared some of his knowledge and counsel with them, assisting them in their development as performers and as people. He also inspired many admirers who identified with his character's problems and looked up to him as a father figure and role model.

Schneider has influenced people through his personal life and philanthropic endeavors in addition to his appearances on screen. Schneider, who has encountered numerous problems and adversities in his life, including injuries, divorces, lawsuits, and the death of his wife, Alicia Allain Schneider, from breast cancer, has always demonstrated perseverance and hope, conquering adversity with grace and faith. He has also used his celebrity and money to give back to the community and support numerous causes, such as the Children's Miracle Network, which he co-founded in 1983 with Marie Osmond and generates donations for children's hospitals around the United States. He has also contributed to disaster relief operations, such as those in response to Hurricane Katrina and the Louisiana floods, and has pushed for animal rights, environmental protection, and veterans' care.

Schneider's legacy is judged not only by his accomplishments and awards, but also by the lives he has touched and hearts he has stirred. He is a living legend whose art and attitude have made a difference in the world. You can say Schneider is a true star who has shone brightly for more than four decades and will continue to inspire generations of fans and artists.

CHAPTER SEVEN

Rare Fun Facts About John Schneider

1. Schneider previously wanted to be a race car driver and attended racing school in Georgia for a short time.

2. To get the breakthrough part of Bo Duke in The Dukes of Hazzard when he was only 18, he acquired a southern accent and lied to filmmakers about being a 24-year-old from Snailville, GA.

3. In 1982, he and Marie Osmond co-founded the Children's Miracle Network, a non-profit organization that raises donations for children's hospitals across the United States.

4. He traded nostalgic presents with Johnny Cash, who gave him a custom duster designed by Manuel and he gave Cash a denim duster fashioned by his great-grandmother.

5. In 2018, he appeared on the popular reality show Dancing with the Stars, where he demonstrated his dancing abilities alongside professional partner Emma Slater.

6. He founded Duke Fest, an annual event that brings together fans of The Dukes of Hazzard from all over the world to honor the show's history.

HEY DEAR READER!

Thank you for taking the time to read this unofficial and brief biography. I hope it was at least an entertaining read with a few lessons. I appreciate your interest.

I also pray that God will bless you in your pockets and in every area of your life. May you flourish and excel in all your pursuits, and may you always have peace and happiness. You are a precious and special person, and you have a great potential and calling.

While we keep getting better, I hope to see you share this book with friends online to enjoy too, and I hope you will read more works from Mia Publications.

Thank you.

Sincerely,
Mia.

Made in the USA
Columbia, SC
11 April 2025